the

MW01598541

©2013
All Rights Reserved

Published in the United States by Bateau Press
www.bateaupress.org

Bateau Press
POB 1584
Northampton, MA
01061

The Bateau Press office is run on the renewable energies
of hydro and wind power.

Printed with soy ink on Mohawk Options PC White
which is made from 100% post consumer waste fiber and
manufactured using wind power.

Typeset in Arno Pro. Titles are Univers.

Covers printed with metallic ink on Mohawk Loop using
letterpress technology from photopolymer plates. Cover
design, letterpress printing, book design and binding by
Shelter Bookworks. www.shelterbookworks.com

ISBN 978-0-9795325-6-6

the frogs are incredibly loud here

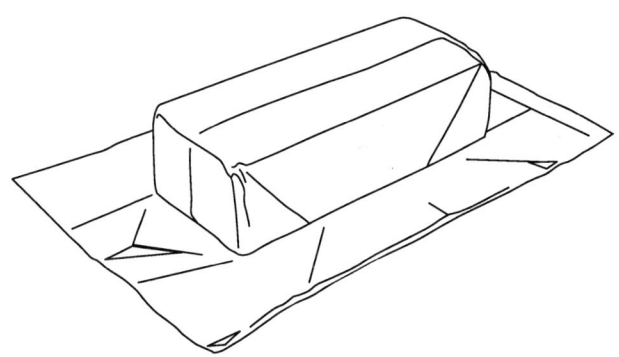

bateau press

Note: Several pieces have appeared in *Juked, Stoked, wigleaf, Corium, NOÖ Journal.*

Contents

"Velveeta is now sold in the United States as a 'Pasteurized Prepared Cheese Product,' a term for which the FDA does not maintain a standard of identity."
The Wall Street Journal

"Don't mess with Mr. In-Between."
Anonymous

Five Painful Memories

1.

Two men in splattered white coats are slaughtering a Velveeta. It screams and screams and screams. Its voice unravels like a yellow stocking thread. I am choking. One man holds a giant gleaming hook with a wooden handle. They are smoking cigars. I run home and refuse to eat my dinner.

2.

They gather on the hill above the library. In the air is the chattering of chainsaw teeth. We all run out into a radish field. In the field are radishes, a purple tent with a red cross on its roof, and further off a Velveeta.

3.

I kiss Sara's fingers. The skin is shiny from the spoon factory. The moon resembles a nest of spiders.

"I'm sorry," she says. "I do love you. But I've given Bobby my Velveeta."

4.

It is hot. I sit in the back row. The sermon is about either lions or leaves. I doodle in the holy book. I lean forward to whisper to L, and my Velveeta tumbles out my shirt pocket. Under everyone's feet, it rolls to the front of the sanctuary! They all turn to me, glaring.

5.

Afterwards the trees resemble question marks. I am in the front yard, in a pile of fresh dirt, playing with my Velveeta. Mother hangs socks from a strand of barbed wire. None of the socks match. A vagabond bangles by. Mother snatches my Velveeta.

"Hey vagabond!" she calls. "Why not come here and take this fat Velveeta?"

In the manner of a feline the vagabond nears the fence. He has a pointy tongue and a nose ring made of a large fishhook. I feel a panic in my throat, then a chilling dread—so this is how it will be. I close my eyes.

Mother laughs. "Ha, I am only joking! Joking! There is nothing else for it, vagabond. Run away."

She hands me back my Velveeta.

Snapshot

Clouds. 7 peppers plastered upon a yellow wheel barrow. Sara's lower back tattoo stretched by hunger. Where do we put the beer? Crisper emptied of plums flung into ceiling fan. Red crockpot on Bobby's head! Hair drips like electric eels lifted from a glazed sea of RO*TEL. Whirling micro waves swarm the air. The apparition of a spoon. Who double-dipped their tranquility? I wonder…On the beads of the bowl TV glitters.

Advice (with Commentary on Cows)

Q: Love seems like a ghost everyone can see, but me. I have capitulated. I just stay at home and brew beer and drink the beer and sterilize the bottles and home-brew again. I am becoming an obsessive compulsive alcoholic. What should I do?

Answers Velveeta: *Box a kangaroo.*

Q: After 30 years of marriage, my husband is more interested in watching Anthony Quinn movies on TV than interacting with me. We are, by mutual consent, no longer intimate—but he totally ignores me. He will talk to anyone who looks his way, but he doesn't talk to me. His idea of doing something together is driving around the countryside for four hours looking at the scenery. He'll lie on the couch and watch TV or read while I'm a few feet away and not say more than a dozen words to me all day. I can't do this much longer.

What do you suggest?

Answers Velveeta: *Grow a beard. Grow a handlebar mustache.*

Q: My young daughter "S" says she wants to be an astronaut, but I fear by the time she's an adult we won't even have any astronauts. What do I tell her?

Answers Velveeta: *Feed three quarters into a Pepsi machine and just walk away.*

> [cows are invented. cows are the darkness. cows stop
> and wait and smell like garlic cloves rubbed into snow
> filling footprints. the exquisite and ugly cow. cows
> beaten with a family stick. cows wallowing along
> the interstate. many-colored birds on the soft backs
> of cows. glass balls blown with bellowing. clattering
> hooves. count the spaces between the ribs of cows.
> carve your spoon. the cow is the cow is the cow.]

12

Q: Don't you think "B" had a responsibility to contact all of his guests and advise them of the problem, and even express concern and apologies?

Answers Velveeta: *Listen, your letter never came.*

> [At this point I left my Writing Chamber and visited the state fair. I required a fried ball of processed cheese and a copy of *The Paris Review*; the cold outside was insufferable. Snow staggered from soggy clouds. We were standing in line. A little girl turned to me.
>
> "Hamburger," she said. "Hamburger comes from cows. People kill the cows and they slice them up into circles and then they eat the circles. They made me eat cow circles but I didn't know what it was," she said sadly. "I didn't know…"
>
> "Please don't start again!" her mother said. She gave me a harsh look like I'd initiated this line of reasoning. "No one meant to taint you. No one knew how you'd feel about it."
>
> "I ate cows," the little girl persisted gravely.
>
> "This is no time to talk about such things!" her mother insisted. She gave me another accusing glare. I glanced down at my feet.
>
> "I just didn't know about the circles," the girl said.]

Q: What is the purpose of life?

Answers Velveeta: *Get tazered.*

Matching Test Question

Instructions:

You have fourteen minutes for this section. Please provide matches for the following three dreams to their dreamer. Some of these dreamers might have more than one dream, while some might have none, so be sure to choose the best answer.

The Dreams:

1. I frantically ride a horse through the streets. Several buoys are stolen from the local harbor, important navigational buoys. Several newspaper stands set aflame. I enter a tavern and black out. The harassment of a badger. Saplings ridden and snapped in half. I spend a great while abstracting energy from various households. I know I feel happy with myself. I feel so happy. I want to grab my imaginary friend and bury him in the mud up to his shoulders and then go and sit upon his head and laugh while eating an apple. My imaginary friend is a toy soldier and wears boxing gloves and I don't like his face, but I like his flame thrower. He has no name. He sleeps in a cage under his bed, inches behind my left ear.

2. A rectangular purse for the carrying of Velveeta, plain, solid black, without ornamentation. (Its skin made from the complicated paperwork necessary to fill out when initiating a legal separation.)

3. Did poetry invent Velveeta, or Velveeta poetry?

The Dreamers:

Sara, Bobby, me.

Childhood

The electricity is shut off (with negligible effect on Velveeta).

Someone throws all of Mother's shoes on the roof, to teach her something.

Sister has a lunch date with a therapist; then later that evening goes swimming with a priest.

Before he cuts loose the enormous, yellow balloon, Father writes us a note: THERE IS NO FREE LUNCH.

Acne scars or battle scars, who is to say?

Bobby drops by, to borrow the doorknobs.

Sara arrives at the back step, a ring of kohl under each eye. She asks for sugar. No sugar exists in this house.

Mother lugs around a shovel.

I walk outside; hold up my open palms to stop the rain. In my stomach, a simpler time, as Velveeta gurgles and sways, much like an angel treading water in a warm gulf, the wavelets pushing small boats into other small boats, the touching and pulling apart. Couples, on grassy hillsides above the harbor, lay out blankets and watch the boats. Often there is dancing. A fat man sells Kool-Aid for a dime, while the children somersault away.

Outside Sister's window, mockingbirds make tidy nests of thong underwear. Like a flower. Like a flower.

But the day is blustery.

Sugarless, Sara turns and walks away.

Below the roof, above the beds, dozens of knives line the attic rafters.

Insulation, Mother murmurs in her sleep.

Review

Over the course of its long career Velveeta has maintained two quite different allegiances. [Sara says, It's been 6 months—when can I quit talking?] With the publication of *Tater Tot Surprise* in 1967, Velveeta brought a bold style and a fresh sense of the numinous to America. [It is what we're dealt.] "The essence flows from the block unbidden," writes Julia Child, "and the hidden source is the soul." The four vertical lines are much shorter than pentameter, as you can smell. Velveeta entertains subjects as diverse as love, death, the effects of marijuana on the creative process, drained chicken, and the full splendor of the flowering self. [I've never in my life seen dissimulation like Bobby had, and I probably never...I mean, it's rare.] On a more solemn note, Velveeta depicts troubled marriage as a dropped bowl of ground beef. But the artist is always a maker of casseroles. [For about a year, I got to thinking, What else am I going to do?] Those greasy crumbles of flesh are picked from ceramic shards, washed carefully under hot water, strained through a coffee filter, and then folded into sour cream and roasted salsa. [Obviously, an event like that...it changed my personality, Sara says.] Velveeta's themes might daunt a lesser artist. Example, from its seminal work, "Slick, Drippy, Stringy, Bubbly (4 Partners Here Renamed):"

slacken

the initial heat

of passion

may refashion.

Anyone? Seconds?

Here is Velveeta at its frequent best—the artist of incipient devourings.

[Sara running, into dull gold light.]

16

From the Opening and Closing Paragraphs of a Note Written Inside the Front Cover of a Book of Poetry (Gary Snyder) and Given to Lost Love

Opening Paragraph:

You were my birthday present; you came to the door—no one else was home. You said, "Let's celebrate." We dropped acid and went to the friend with the nocturnal monkey-like animal and made Velveeta for hours.

Closing Paragraph:

Today we are with different lovers. Mostly I feel bloated and murky. My eyes are murky because that's all I see, murky streets and murky fields and murky everything. Did you know that whales often explode? They do, go look it up. Mostly it's beached whales and all the people standing around with their cameras or whatever and then the whale explodes. I find it horrible and fascinating and true. You know, that last day I did not cry. I let our Velveeta be universal. "Don't take it personally," you said. I told you maybe I liked being murky and morose. Maybe I should be named Velveeta crying something. You bring up from inside me the sorrows and pains of loss. We try to accept them, but they are as real as the taut skin of an overripe whale. That's where I was going with the whole whale thing, if you were wondering. In these times, I'm not sure the world needs metaphors anymore, but I do. I need metaphors. They help me. I carry you with me still and always will—until death.

Velveeta Crying Something

Nine Translations of *Mirlitonnades* by Samuel Beckett (With Quotations of Judy Garland)

Velveeta on and on Velveeta on (my translation) all life one Velveeta to coin a scheme whereby in time to rhyme it all into a single jingle (translation by Judy Garland) Velveeta causes anything to be something to be anything so that, let us say, one both is and is not (translation by Sara) Saturday's reprieve no Velveeta after midnight before midnight (translation by Bobby) Velveeta without cease or treaty of peace (translation by Bobby)

> [Quotations of Judy Garland:
> Behind every cloud is another cloud.
> I think there's something peculiar about me that I haven't died.
> I was born at the age of twelve.
> When I walk onstage you should hear my balls clank.
> I believe in the idea of the rainbow. And I've spent my entire life trying to get over it.
> If I am a legend, then why am I so lonely?
> I am a chemist. I know what pills I am taking!
> The most nightmarish feeling in the world is suddenly to feel like throwing up in front of four thousand people.
> At least one wall is shaking.
> There is fat and there is bloat.
> I've either been an enormous success or just a down-and-out failure.
> I'm not drunk. I am glazed.
> I want to finish this, do you mind?]

aspire Velveeta forever never retire (translation by Bobby) Velveeta without break asleep or awake (translation by Bobby) words of Velveeta survive this life brief companions (translation by Sara.)

On Writing About…

—It cannot be done.

—You are fishing in a crisper drawer. (Your fishing pole is an anthropologist.)

—Velveeta does not need a writer to be understood. Any human—unless willfully ignorant or just stubborn for stubbornness sake, like a mule or a ball of unraveled twine in a kitchen junk drawer (its looping patterns often resembling the meanderings of a housefly stimulated by a drop of sugar water)—can perfectly understand Velveeta. But what about Velveeta's *value*? To grasp what is unique and irreplaceable in its contributions? To articulate the previously unknown attributes of existence Velveeta has discovered? Well, possibly we need a writer…like Sean Lovelace. Possibly, the writings of Sean Lovelace, however haphazard his thinking, however riddled (shall we say addled?) his mind, if still supported by true passion (who here can say otherwise?) can, or possibly will, maintain its usefulness, as words may provoke and engender additional thinking and thereby assist in constituting a *meditation*, an intellectual foundation, a series of critical echoes, a background essential to the greater understanding of Velveeta, and in doing so—

> [At this point I left my Writing Chamber. I walked to the library to continue my research. A square, green, sputtering machine roared to a halt. A woman opened the door. Within her eyes, a circus.
>
> "The fuck you doing?" she yelled.
>
> "Huh?"
>
> "You walked right across the grass! Walk on the sidewalks, not the grass."
>
> "I'm sorry," I said.

19

"Sorry doesn't grow grass!" She slammed shut the door on the green cube and caterwhomped away.

The day was miserably hot. Sweat pooled along my waistline. I felt just a little bit shorter, as if *de-cruited*, or *de-growing*. I wanted to say to the circus woman; I wanted to say, "Human nature is not my fault. If I was the architect of this town, or any town, I would have built everything first but the sidewalks and let the people walk—let them express their mortal sensibilities of awareness and direction and tendency—and once a few months had passed, once their natural meanderings/shortcuts and joyful lollygags/struts and stretches and ways of life had worn gentle paths in the grass, I would have *then* paved over the paths, to create walkways where the people already wanted to walk. Now why can't life be that way?"

But I didn't say any of that. Having lost my momentum, I faced about and returned to my Writing Chamber.]

—It's a mechanical contraption. Why must you remind us?

—Writing transforms Velveeta into historical fact. To create a Velveeta around Velveeta. Blur. Shape, fashion, form, mold.

—The great thing about yellow is that it isn't black and isn't white.

—Some of us want to know *less* about *more*, OK?

—Have I mentioned the usefulness of the box?

[—What do you want me to say? I'll say it.

—I don't want you to say anything.

—Right. That's the truth right there. I feel it acutely.]

—Plasticity of emotion.

—(Human need for sensation.)

—Oh my.

Oh, it Lives

in a music-box of crooked smiles. In the crumbly eyes of toasted cheese
Virgin Mary (eBay: $28,000). Spat or spot or shat, Velveeta is composed
of lava lamp, the shape that is light, the slip of pink, the blob, I mean to say
emotions. (*Strenuous*, our lives. If we could only find our...) Velveeta is a
curb feeler, a throbbing kiss, a scratch or pick, a time Mom screeched at Dad,
ripped at his thin, shimmery self-esteem/the steering wheel—*crash!* (Recoil
funky: fashion of facial scars.) But what about the child and the bicycle?
What bicycle? And Mom liked to doodle palm trees onto bible pages and
to name herself *guest host* [exquisite oxymoron] and would faint in crowds,
so lay off Mom. Dad is in the basement with the basement. An alternative to
hugs—why not try squeezing marshmallows? (Oh, we are funny, but not ha-
ha funny.) Velveeta lives in cellphones. Also in muck. Ok, a playful straddle of
cellphones and muck. It makes its presence in the moments of those wading
upstream, pushing their wrapped, crinkly bundles: pelvic butter and jars of
humiliation; bouncy checks and whiplash; flickering lights, fumble fingers,
mouths like staple-guns. We awake in the stomach of the night. Velveeta is
our recurring dream. [I may or may not purchase my first bed. I'm sleeping on
it...] Huge! Illuminated! Expiration date unknown.

Sex Life

Most days crows perch outside the large windows and ignore Velveeta. Dogs treat Velveeta in one of three ways: 1. Stare it down snarling. 2. Sniff, wait, sniff, sniff, wait…lick away. 3. Slumber.

Two hundred and fifty catastrophes. Touching a sore spot, for example. Unflattering noise. Locks that do not lock. Protesters hiding in armpits and various throats. Multiple passwords. Multiple aftershocks. Never enough salt, for the triangles. Bobby's ex-wife who kicked Velveeta while dying. People who refuse the dying, who play coy.

Mirror says in pearly clatter, "Looks like this is going to take all night."

The pebble and the water and the grit. The brick. Power shortages. Audacity while the television smells of suffering. Twitters of toilet paper.

Hung in the shape of Q, these other ones. The Makeup Man. The cookbook. Bobby's new girlfriend. The curious reporters (see dogs above). The girlfriend who wept about airstrikes while sorting the tortilla chips. The girlfriend who closed her eyes. The girlfriend who blogged Velveeta, live. The slippery phone. What to make of this buzzing? Kicking left and right andbackwards simultaneously. EXIT signs. Bobby's boss and the boss's wife.

The brick oven. Slatted oval windows and vents. Mudslides of air and light. Joint statements.

Example: One day I show up spectacularly drunk with a love poem and throw it hard into Velveeta. I pull and I pull, but I can't pull it out.

Just another conversation.

The cleaning of the oven and the dirtying of the oven.

23

He opens the door for Sara. She peers inside and says, "I see already this room has many rooms."

If you just squint your eyes…

Outside the windows, the crows. They suggest, *Kill the lights.*

Balcony

Velveeta sun on the horizon, all smeared-out sliding gold. Reminds me of Dad, who melted away. Hey Dad, are you eating Velveeta right now? I don't think so. Some type of giant rodent crosses the courtyard and shakes its head slowly. The drinks are weak. The seagulls nosy. The pineapple, neither apple nor pine. The ocean is the ocean and the breeze will not stop blowing. Look at my windbreaker, tourist yellow. The same yellow found boiling in glass tubes, Monroe, New York, 1918. Emil Frey is inventing Velveeta! Sweet odors of turnip oil, saffron, minced copper, sweat. Sweet whisper of a Bunsen burner. The frogs are incredibly loud here, Dad. It feels like they are squatting inside my head. They screech *yeell-ow, yeell-ow*. The streetlight smudge. Coughing taxicab. Emil walks his way home. Stops for his customary two drinks. Shakes salt into the beer. Drops by the five-and-dime for oranges. (He still can't get over the oranges.) Buys an orange and a thimble and a tinned ham. Pauses in the hissing snow. Turns back to get the yo-yo.

From *Interview Magazine*, March, 1970

Q: Does this country not like serious Velveeta?

A: No, it doesn't. You're not supposed to think in America. It's good to think in Portugal, in Switzerland—people accept it. In America, to think is something horrible, and so people hate you, they spit in your face. That's what they did to me for years. The only person that didn't spit in my face was Sean Lovelace, except that Sean Lovelace loves to keep his Velveeta at home. He loves to sit quietly and look at Velveeta. You know, he's a broken man. Like much of the world, he's full of regret and sadness. Velveeta is an excellent salve for regret and sadness. But, if there's no distribution, there is of course no impact. I like him I suppose; he's an adequate artist, but Sean Lovelace is in love with his Velveeta and stores it in his bedroom, some even under his bed!

From "Obliterating Velveeta with Explosives," a pamphlet issued by the Recreation and Sanitation Program of the U.S. Department of Health and Human Services

There are times when it is important to obliterate Velveeta from locations such as recreation areas where Velveeta might attract scoundrels, at a popular water fountain where the public might object, or along the shoulders of roads or hotel entrances. Explosives have successfully been used by qualified blasters to partially or totally obliterate Velveeta. It is important to consider location, time of year, and size of Velveeta when selecting the quantity and type of explosive to accomplish the obliteration task. The following instructions pertain to partial obliteration (dispersion) for Velveeta that weighs about 1,100 pounds. In this first example, urgency is not a factor— perhaps the public is feeling low and is not expected to visit the area for several days, or perhaps scoundrels will be scant at best due to environmental degradation. In any case, in this example, dispersion is acceptable. Place three pounds of explosives under Velveeta in four locations. Velveeta can then be rolled onto the explosives if necessary. Place one pound of explosives on each end of the rectangular block. Use detonator cord to tie the explosives' charges together. Metallic wrapping should be removed to minimize dangerous flying debris. In situations where total Velveeta obliteration is necessary, it is advisable to double the amount of explosives. Total obliteration might be preferred in situations where the public is expected in the area the next day (an angry, politicized mob or a sale on lingerie, for example), or where scoundrels are particularly prolific. Velveeta that has been dispersed will generally be vaguely remembered within a few days. Velveeta that has been obliterated will generally not show any trace of having existed at all.

The Naturalist

A teenager tosses a turkey sandwich into a boiling, sulfurous pool. She takes six photos: her face, dripping cliffs, her inner thigh, a T-shirt stand, a giant yellow hotel, her face. Two of the photos she texts away.

Ten minutes before the opening remarks, the supply closet door opens and there I stand, The Velveeta Naturalist. I cough. The odor of urine and beer and Pine Sol. I hold a can of Budweiser in each hand.

—Who is you? says the maid.

—I'm sorry…I always have stage fright.

A morning stroll along the trails above the hotel. Gurgling tributaries of steam. A clearing holds a blue tent and a poodle tied to a picnic table. The tent wobbles like a sock of marbles. Grunts and groans. On impulse, I walk up to the dog and untie its leash. The poodle runs into the forest. Later, I see (and make a sketching of) my first Pet Rock in the wild.

A little boy stands in the lobby with his eyes shut and thinks, "No one can find me now."

A pair of underwear is sucked into a windstorm and blown out into the quiet suburbs. Someone says, "I'm dizzy." A crow recruits a mockingbird into its murder.

A murmuring of various flushed toilets.

Men of yellowing skin sit on whitewashed stairways. They rub their fingers together and watch the streets for dropped dollar bills and cleavage. The sun moves along the clouds or the clouds along the sun, in flickering rays, like a wind-up toy projector. A squirrel nibbles a French fry.

The Velveeta Graduate Student stands naked in Bobby's room and examines a tablet of Oxycontin. Little quivering moon. She examines it into halves, then examines it into crumbles—chop/chop/chop—and eventually examines it into a fine, brown powder and right up her nose. A cell phone buzzes on the floor.

Sara stirs in the bathtub, emitting a little moan. Bobby throws a large cat and a mint julep off the balcony.

The door opens again! *What are you doing here?* Bobby rips away my name tag and slams and locks the door...

"Regarding the uses of Velveeta," The Velveeta Naturalist says, "it is one of the means by which the hue of yellow is transported from coral reef and edge of star, to be deposited far inland where it otherwise would never prosper. Velveeta also greatly mitigates the extremes of spastic movement. By day Velveeta shields various crevasses from the scorching influence of the heat. Postulations abound that Velveeta allows us to avoid becoming even further what we already are. Benefits arising from Velveeta are felt in every country, every land, every sea, or even fathomless archipelago or disco. Lastly, whether we contemplate Velveeta with respect to its color, its aroma, its tongue-feel, its numerous modifications, or, more than all, its incessant state of change, this 'phenomenon' proves a source of never-failing interest, and may be classed among the most beautiful manifestations in the natural universe."

Applause.

Might I Interest You in a Box?

A simple, honest, rectangular wooden box. I emphasize the word, *honest*. Or contemplate this: its form has no direct model in nature. Just the thought of such a shape, much less the actual construction of, is true testament to man's potential capacity. The same could be said, of course, about its former contents: Velveeta. Ever felt you are devoid a dimension? Listen: following some act of darkness, as you kneel vomiting into the curbside, a galaxy is stirring above your sweating brow. Oh, your fragile, threatened expression. This is about Bobby, isn't it? A tooth sunk into the muscle of your existence, I get that. Like with Sara. I get all of that. Sara is like the stars that burn all day, though we only see them at night—that's how it is exactly. An absence always present. A paradox. Well, this box is waiting to be filled. You could dwell inside it quite comfortably. To express that you recognize but are different than the angels. There is no recorded incident of an angel living in a box. Angels have no need, but we are not angels. Clearly. A box is orderly. You are stating, I am orderly. Storage? To hold onto certain keepsakes. Material effects that trigger memory. A napkin, sea glass, maybe the severed hand of a childhood toy. First aid kits? Various precautionary tools. Who knows what the future may bring? What if someone yells out, "Gas! Gas! Quick boys!" Where are you going to run? We are all in need of shelter, right? Install a few shelves and this box becomes a reliable bookcase, or a beer rack! Yes, you have that look. So, while you are alive, a beer rack, a bookcase. Visitors will see this box and think, *style, wow, vintage.* You will become as interesting as a panther, yet still with a sense of rationality, as you stand straight, alongside the upright box. And when you die? Yes, I've said it, when you die. Listen: this box becomes your final resting place. Now, just listen. While you're using the box for all the books and the beer and the firearms, etc., the wooden top just hangs off the back—we can install a few hinges. When you die, the box closes. We'll secure the lid with maple pins. I know, I know: why would I want a coffin while alive? Good question. But death is an inevitable part of life. Buying a box now can help begin a process of education and acceptance: by seeing your wooden box every day, you will be reminded of the preciousness of physical life. And when all is said and done, when Bobby and Sara vanish into what they always truly were—dreams or a long nightmare or no more than the hazy blue stirrings before you fall asleep—you can rest peacefully, knowing that you are enclosed in a Velveeta box to which you have added significant personal meaning. So. What do you think?

Of All the Possible Processed Cheese

Dedicated to poet and actor, Deter Pavis

1. Velveeta
One idea is this. When you begin discussing the finer details in place of
Every important Velveeta you substitute the word, Velveeta. This Velveeta
Becomes the game to the extent that discussing some other Velveeta thought
Or Velveeta idea is obviously now Velveeta. For instance, as I'm writing here
Now I move along, forward so to speak in a rectangular motion until Velveeta.
It's as simple as that. When one Velveeta ends, a new Velveeta begins and thus
All Velveeta is the same Velveeta. For the purposes of this moment, I'm speaking
Of Velveeta's Velveeta. Whose name I would whisper were it not for the Velveeta
Which holds my belt in place. That one lynchpin that directs the complete
Velveeta or arches an eyebrow over a lover's Velveeta.

2. Rectangle
In the second place, we must consider the rectangle that is rectangle. Of course,
A lined rectangle, lined with the very metallic sheen of Velveeta. Suppose this
Is step two and the covers of your bed become rectangle and your dreams get
Rectangle and your rectangle becomes rectangle. Let's think about all of this for
A moment. A rectangle Velveeta is the place you put the pit of your stomach. A
Rectangle pail of water is the rectangle Velveeta you put the pit of your stomach.
On rectangle knees, rectangle. And at night.

3. Yellow
Which precedes the argument yellow. Yellow is the yellow that replaces all
Yellow. Yellow is the ribbon. Yellow is the government. Yellow is the yellow in
The back of our yellowed yellow. This idea, coupled with various instances of
Processed cheese (mainly, Velveeta) and rectangleness, configured or, if you
Like, melted on an upper yellow. Apparently, even if we were to arrive at the end
Of language we'd find the relatively small area below the yellow. We could nearly
Yellow the yellow and nearly smell it too. Under these circumstances, given the
Century's attention to yellow and yellowness and all of the various possibilities
Of yellow. In one instance, on one occasion, we experienced the particular
Configuration of yellow rectangle yellow. Of yellow, rectangle, Velveeta.

Thuds on the Roof

In the dark. It shimmers in its wobble. Nothing between but the cooling itch of shingle. It admires any angle or gravity suck. To embrace sway. It wants to push against itself—much like we. (Yesterday, sober, I dropped a wine glass of Cheetos and laughed at my own sudden blood. Under sink/in trunk of car/beneath futon—I keep no hand towels.) On the back of its neck, thoughts gleam. It boasts its mind is a butterfly ashtray. As for doubt or nocturnal chills of the head, it claims to know very little. Yet it corrects me: shooting stars are not stars, you ask for shotgun slugs never bullets, to fall over is indeed a form of exercise. Oh, the type to wear an orange shirt. To perch above my Sunday sweating back and say cryptic, unhelpful words, like "If you are really going to dig that hole, dig two." Or maybe: "Look at you, whipjack! Gargling coins again." Packages arrive. Days of fingernail tapping rain. It sees me on my knees, vomiting in the tall, wet grass and says, "You are an empty tomato shack." I think its mind is an ashtray full of butterflies. (Ah, so drunk now. Just to carry my head like a goddamn fiddler. A marble spinning round the rim of shattered glass, waxy hot pepper bits, dulled knives, charred *documents*—I mean to say the kitchen sink. *What is a tomato shack?*) A meteor claws the fleshy sky. In the dark. Velveeta thuds off the roof.

A Scale of Massive Wind

Level:

1. Bricks fall from chimneys.

2. Bobby says he doesn't care for Sara's peach.

3. Where did the birds go?

4. Stained and silvered Velveeta wrappings resemble rainfall.

5. Graceless and dumbfounded with desire, I hand dip candles. I wrap them into tissue paper, into a shoebox. I wait for the perfect moment, sitting all day, moment upon moment, waiting.

6. Bobby shows Sara his brand new talking toilet.

7. Moving autos are pushed off the roads.

8. Due to a series of ingenious levers and helical springs, the original wooden Velveeta box was far roomier than appearance and, in times of need, could accommodate numerous celebrities and their personal interests. (For example: Richard Burton holding generous parties for the local football club. Steve McQueen steadying Sara's surfboard. Bert and Ernie opening a co-op supermarket. Katherine Hepburn drinking gin from a lava lamp. Woody Allen tickling a naval officer. Lily Tomlin sharing tea with Secretariat. Secretariat smoking a cigarette [actually rolled newsprint and never lit].)

9. Shelves empty of bread, milk, hair conditioner.

10. I compliment Sara's peach, but she doesn't hear. Bobby buys Sara a martini the size of an elevator. A dozen olives bob.

11. Phones become missiles.

12. Bobby visits me.

> [—What's on TV?
>
> —I am alone on this planet and I don't even know where I belong.
>
> —The fuck that means? The Weather Channel?]

13. Trains tumble over.

14. Clouds *thump*.

15. Libraries explode.

16. Clattering wooden spoons blot out the sky.

17. I feel the rippling fabric of the soul lifting from my bones.

18. Bobby gnashes!

19. Inconceivable. (If this level is ever achieved, evidence might only be found in some manner of ground swirl pattern, for it may never be identifiable through engineering studies.)

20. Sara is gone.

bateau press

BATEAU PRESS publishes chapbooks and
the annual magazine, *Bateau*.

Sean Lovelace's *The Frogs are Incredibly Loud Here*
won the 2013 BOOM Chapbook Contest.